Morning Blessings & Mercies

A 30-Day Devotional on the Gospel Fulfilling Your Walk in His Purpose

By: Tony Mejia

A 30-DAY DEVOTIONAL ON THE GOSPEL FULFILLING YOUR WALK IN HIS PURPOSE

Morning Blessing & Mercies

BY; TONY MEJIA

3

Other Books of Tony Mejia English and Spanish

1. From The Streets to The Altar
2. A Journey to Redemption

Spanish:
1. De Las Calles al Altar
2. El Camino A la Redención

Books Written by Tony Mejia wife Heidy Mejia

1. Beyond my Wounds
2. The Power of Forgiveness

Spanish:
1. Mas Alla de Mis Heridas
2. El Poder del Perdón

Introduction:

Greetings from a graceful and purposeful journey of transformation! We begin a holy journey in the quiet of the morning, just as the sun is softly awakening the earth. This 30-day journey will explore heavenly favors, infinite mercies, and the tremendous influence of the Gospel on your life's perspective.

We discover a hallowed place where the beat of our hearts and the whispered words of eternity collide in the quiet of dawn. "Morning Blessings & Mercies" is an invitation to experience the live Gospel and a close walk with the Savior, whose mercies are new every morning, rather than merely a devotional.

Every devotion you have over these 30 days together is like a line of paint on the canvas of your spirit, done with the bright colors of the promises of God, His direction, and the bright brightness of His purpose. This devotional is not just a daily reading; it's a heavenly conversation, an investigation into the richness of your identity in Christ, and an illumination of His purpose as it is being revealed to you every day.

Anticipate being uplifted, challenged, and changed. Every day provides a key to reveal a different aspect of how the Gospel affects your path.

"Good morning, Blessings & Mercies" is a ray of hope that points you toward the unwavering bedrock of God's love, regardless matter whether you are living in the shadows of unknowing or the morning of gladness.

Let the gospel be your constant companion, the words of this devotional serve as your guide, and the morning serve as your haven. I pray that this 30-day journey will fill your life with the abundance of God's favor, the deliciousness of His kindness, and the steadfast confidence that comes from following His plan. May you find the grace to complete the path in His glorious artwork each morning.

"Knowing who you are in Christ is a journey of change where your identity fits with the perfection that God created you to be. It's not just a revelation."

We frequently see our physical selves reflected in the mirror, but how often do we consider the image of God that resides within us? Let's start our devotional journey by accepting who you are in Christ. You are a purposeful work of art made in the exact likeness of your Creator; you are not an accidental creation. God has a purpose for you; you are more than just a creature. You are invited to proclaim His praises and shine His light in a world in need of hope as a vessel of His love and grace.

You and Christ are co-heirs as God's children, not just heirs. Your identity is entwined with the majesty of Christ; you participate in His final victory even as you share in His sorrows.

The mental process of realizing who you are in Christ requires mental alteration. God urges you to refresh your thinking in accordance with His truth, even though the world may define you by other people's standards.

Your identity in Christ is a garment, a coat of righteousness, not only an idea. Recall that you are covered by Christ's grace while you proceed on your spiritual path.

Reflection:
Today, take a time to gaze in the mirror and see not only your outward appearance but also the soul that God has so carefully crafted. Keep in mind that you bear your Heavenly Father's magnificent imprint as you look in the mirror. How does your personality affect how you view obstacles and successes?

Prayer:
Lord, please open my eyes so I can see myself the way You do. Assist me in accepting the fact that You created me in Your image, fearfully and beautifully.

"So, God created mankind in his own image, in the image of God he created them." - NIV, Genesis 1:27

"Without the coverings from your life is an act of weakness, permitting the real beauty of your soul to come to light and reveal the transformative impact of God's grace."

Although it is encouraged of us as Christians to live according to Christ's virtues, we frequently build up layers that hide who we really are. Let's start the process of removing the layers that conceal our true selves now. It can be difficult to wear the perfectionism mask. Let's examine the freedom that comes from letting go of the need for perfection and accepting God's grace in our imperfections.

We frequently hide our fear under a veneer of self-preservation. Let's examine the ability and love that God offers to remove the fear mask. Comparing frequently results in the addition of a mask, concealing our actual selves behind the achievements or outward manifestations of others. Let's discover the fulfillment that comes from our individual journey today.

Reflection:
Consider the qualities listed in Colossians 3:12. Think about any more layers or masks you could have inadvertently added to your genuine identity. How can you find fulfillment and freedom in accepting your special journey?

Prayer:
Lord, show me the layers I've put on top of my life. Give me the strength to eliminate everything that prevents me from truly reflecting Your image.

"Therefore, as God's chosen people, holy and dearly loved, clothe yourselves with compassion, kindness, humility, gentleness and patience." - NIV Colossians 3:12

"The vision of the Lord is not just a blueprint; it's a divine layout, deeply woven into the very fabric of your being, waiting to be revealed as you accept what God planned you to be."

The plan that God had for your life began even before you were born. Let's examine the certainty that you were made with a purpose and that there is hope in God's intentions. Let's explore the idea that you were meticulously created by God for a specific purpose today. God's plan for your life is revealed via your faith. Let's examine today how fulfilling God's divine plan requires faith in both His existence and His promises. Your life is shaped and molded by God, the Potter. The resignation that is required to be malleable in His hands and to allow Him to shape you in accordance with His divine plan. Living in accordance with God's will is living in His vision. Let's investigate today how we can give thanks to God and live each day in the name of Jesus.

Reflection:

Let go of the notion that God has a predetermined course for your life. How does realizing this affect the way you view your mission and the future?

Prayer:

"Lord, I am grateful for Your intentions for my life." Please give me hope for the future You have planned for me and help me to trust in Your purpose.

"For I know the plans I have for you, declares the Lord, plans for welfare and not for evil, to give you a future and a hope." - ESV Jeremiah 29:11

"The Balance of growing periods is an art of combining tolerance with development, allowing the foundations of wisdom to grow deeper while the branches of your abilities reach for new levels."

Seasons affect nature, and they also affect our spiritual and personal development. Let's examine the meaning of the seasons today and how they enhance the splendor of our voyage. Perseverance is the seed that keeps us going through every growing season. Let's consider the value of patience as we work toward becoming the people that God has intended us to be. Pruning is a crucial component of development. Let's consider how God's gentle pruning prepares us to bear more fruit in His kingdom.

There may be periods of excess and scarcity throughout growth seasons. Let's consider the lessons we take away from both experiences today and how they help us be happy. Transformation is the aim of growth seasons. Let's consider today how growing in Christlikeness is a result of every season.

Reflections:
Think about the phase of life you are in right now. What facets of development and transformation are you going through?

Prayer:
Lord, please enable me to identify and welcome whatever season I'm in. Give me the discernment to recognize the value that every season adds to my journey.

"There is a time for everything, and a season for every activity under the heavens." - 3:1 in Ecclesiastes (NIV)

"God's grace produces powerful smudges turning the blank page of our daily existence into an incredible work of salvation, where every line speaks the story of God everlasting love."

The canvas of our souls is painted with vivid hues of forgiveness by the grace of God. Let us consider the extent of forgiveness provided by His boundless grace. The grace of God transforms as well as pardons. Let's investigate the notion that His grace acts as a paintbrush, transforming us into a brand-new work of art. God's unfailing love is manifested in His grace. Let's consider the loving craftsmanship that was on exhibit today in Jesus' selfless deed.

Let's consider the continual process of growing in God's grace as we come to an end. His boundless grace is like a painter constantly shaping our lives into something beautiful.

Reflection:
Consider a moment when you felt pardoned by God. What effects did it have on your relationships and life?

Prayer:
Lord, I am grateful for Your grace, which includes forgiveness. May Your mercy's hues permeate every aspect of my life.

"You have been saved by grace through faith. Furthermore, this is a gift from God; it is not anything you did." - (ESV) Ephesians 2:8

Day 6

" Recognizing your own distinctive pattern is the glorious submission to the Creator's motive, accepting the unique lines of the heart that create the finished product of your reality."

Let's start our devotional journey with recognizing that you are a masterpiece created by God, perfectly engineered for a specific purpose. Your unique style is deliberate and in line with God's purpose for your life. You were made in God's likeness. You are special and valued because of the way that your unique design embodies His divine qualities. God deserves appreciation for his design. Consider the fact that you are a masterpiece of His amazing handiwork—fearfully and beautifully crafted.

Both your talents and shortcomings are part of your unique design. Let us examine the grace of accepting both, understanding that Christ's strength is made perfect in our infirmities. As we come to an end, keep in mind that God is still working in you. Step out with assurance, knowing that He will keep reshaping and molding your unique creation.

Reflection:
Think about the fact that you are a creation of God. What impact does this viewpoint have on how you perceive your mission?

Prayer:
Heavenly Father, I am grateful that You created me with a purpose. Assist me in finding and accomplishing the good deeds You have planned for me.

"For we are God's handiwork, created in Christ Jesus to do good works, which God prepared in advance for us to do." - NIV Ephesians 2:10

"The strength of God's affection is not just a strength; it's a great creator, molding the forms of your heart, shaping you into the wonder and compassion you were created to be."

Let's go out on a journey to discover the power of God's love today. His love is fundamental and not based on our deservingness; it is exemplified by Christ's self-sacrificing deed on the cross. Our identity is transformed by God's love, which grants us the status of His children. Let's consider the significant implications of being referred to as God's children.

Let's investigate the relationship between His love and the alteration of our mental habits. Let's consider how fear can be conquered by His flawless love. Love is a catalyst for love in our own lives; it is not only something we receive. Let's consider how His love enables us to love others.

Reflection:
Examine the riches of God's love as shown in Romans 5:8. How has realizing His love for us while we were still sinners affected your sense of value?

Prayer:
Heavenly Father, I am grateful that You showed me Your love by sending Christ to die on the cross. Assist me in realizing the extent of Your unwavering love for me.

"But God demonstrates his own love for us in this: While we were still sinners, Christ died for us."
- NIV, Romans 5:8

Day 8

"Our imperfections are not marks on Christ; rather, they are chances for His redeeming work. Instead of erasing our flaws, He redeems them and uses our brokenness to create an image of His grace.

Start your devotional journey by realizing that Christ's strength is seen in our frailties and infirmities. Consider accepting imperfection as a chance to let God's grace show. Our imperfections can be hidden and transformed by God's love. Consider the thought that love transforms us into vessels of His favor by acting as a purifying fire. We are defined by His redemptive story, not by our imperfections, in Christ. Consider the fresh creation that results from giving Him our imperfections.

A useful strategy for getting over shortcomings is repentance. Today, consider God's grace that results in purification by sincere repentance. As you wrap up this devotional, keep in mind that you will always triumph over your weaknesses in Christ. Consider how grateful we are for Christ's ability to improve our lives.

Reflection:
Identify a flaw or weakness that you find difficult. What role might God's power and grace play there?

Prayer:
Lord, I am grateful for Your ample grace. Assist me in accepting my shortcomings, understanding that Your strength is enhanced by them.

However, he told me, 'My power is made perfect in weakness, so my grace is sufficient for you.'" I shall thus happily boast about my shortcomings in order to let Christ's strength to rest on me." - NIV, 2 Corinthians 12:9

"Combining the glory of God into everyday life is a way of identifying His presence in the regular, converting ordinary times into an arena where His splendor produces an amazing work of divine value."

Commence your spiritual journey by recognizing God's ever-present presence in your life. Consider acknowledging His magnificence in the routine parts of your day. Gratitude allows you to incorporate God's glory throughout your day and the mercies of the Lord. Give thanks for all of life's blessings, large and little. Our love for each other is how God's splendor is revealed. Consider how you might show everyone around you that you reflect His love.

Seek God's wisdom when making decisions to integrate His glory. Consider giving your plans to Him today and putting your faith in His boundless knowledge. Consider how you can shine God's light throughout the earth. Think about the ways you can spread His light today by being kind, giving, and compassionate.

Reflection:
Try to think of a daily task when you can consciously feel God's presence. How might you view things differently now that you know this?

Prayer:
Heavenly Father, please help me to always recognize Your presence. May I recognize Your closeness and see Your splendor in the everyday.

"Where is your Spirit leading me? Where can I get away from you?" - NIV Psalm 139:7

Day 10

"Putting confidence in God's period of your growth is a step of faith that enables the seeds that have the potential to grow into a beautiful garden, created by the hands of the Lord."

Commence your contemplative journey by appreciating the beauty that results from God's impeccable timing. Think on the knowledge that He is the one who oversees every stage of your life right now. Incorporate optimism while you wait. Consider the relationship between exercising patience and placing your faith in God's promises. Have faith in God's growth plan for you.

Meditate on His plans include promise and a future that is beyond your comprehension. Keep your composure while you await development. Consider the connection between patience and hope as you let God's timing work itself out. Give up your desire for control and put your faith in the guidance of God. Consider giving up your knowledge to His wisdom now so that you might continue your path of development.

Reflection:
Think back to a moment when you were eager to grow. How might your heart be at rest if you trusted in God's timing?

Prayer:
"Thank You, Heavenly Father, for Your divine timing." Please help me to trust that everything will become beautiful in due time.

"He has made everything beautiful in its time." - NIV Ecclesiastes 3:11

"The precious brilliance of forgiveness from God is like a beautiful stained-glass window, piecing together what is broken with shades of grace, generating an intricate work of restoration that reflects God's infinite love."

Start your spiritual journey by realizing that brokenness is brittle. Consider the delicate beauty that might arise as we give God our brokenness today. Consider the creative nature of forgiveness. Examine the notion that God's pardon is not just a gift but also a call to share that grace with people. Examine the restorative hues of God's pardoning. Consider the ability of His grace to heal the scars of a broken heart.

Think about the picture of redemption that God's pardoning has painted. Consider the abundance of His grace that results in our salvation. As you wrap up this devotional, think about the delicate beauty at work. Consider how forgiveness—both given and received—becomes a sign of God's ability to transform today.

Reflection:
Think back to a time when something in your life broke. How many that weakness become a canvas for God's grace if He were to pardon it?

Prayer:
Gracious Father, please create a heart of righteousness in me despite my brokenness. Please revitalize me, and may Your pardon serve as the cornerstone for my recovery.

"Create in me a pure heart, O God, and renew a steadfast spirit within me." - NIV Psalm 51:10

Day 12

"Cultivating a mentality of gratitude is like looking to a field of appreciation; with each mindful plant of generosity, you develop the ground of your heart, allowing the fruits of fulfillment to flourish."

Begin your spiritual journey by giving thanks for today's gift. Think on how beautiful the moment is right now and all the reasons you may be grateful for it. Consider being happy in the little things. Acknowledge the power of God in the little things in life and give thanks for the minor blessings that frequently go unrecognized. Investigate thankfulness in hardship. Think about how you may change your viewpoint today by learning to be grateful even during difficult circumstances. Think about valuing other people. Make a conscious effort to thank and support someone within your life today.

Reflection:

Examine the distinctive features of the present day. How might you become more conscious of God's blessings if you were to cultivate an attitude of gratitude?

Prayer:

"Heavenly Father, I am grateful for today's blessing." Let me appreciate Your creation and let me see its beauty and opportunities.

"This is the day that the Lord has made; let us rejoice and be glad in it." - ESV Psalm 118:24

"Having faith in the purposes of God during difficulty is like discovering a rock of hope in the rough storm of uncertainty—a firm belief that transforms obstacles into stories of divine destiny."

Start this devotional day by recognizing God's sovereignty. Today the promise that His plan is ultimately successful, even during adversity. Contemplate acquiring a more elevated viewpoint. Reflect on how God's ways are beyond our comprehension and provide insight and knowledge throughout difficult circumstances. Consider putting your faith in His immutability.

Think about the security that comes from understanding Christ never changes and can always be relied upon to provide a strong base when things are tough. Those who trust in God in difficult times find safety in His goodness and faithfulness. As you wrap up this devotional, concentrate on the certainty of His purpose. Consider how God promises to bring prosperity, hope, and security for the future regardless of the midst of difficulties.

Reflection:

Think back to a circumstance that is bringing you problems in your life. In what ways could accepting God's sovereignty be consoling and encouraging?

Prayer:

Almighty God, I am grateful for Your omnipotent design. Please strengthen my faith in Your plan, especially in the face of difficulty.

"Many are the plans in a person's heart, but it is the Lord's purpose that prevails." - NIV Proverbs 19:21

"Uncovering your spiritual gifts is an understanding of God's personal tool inside you—a supernatural gift that, when discovered, permits you to add distinctively to the perfection of God existence."

Start your spiritual trip by thinking about a high point of view. Consider the fact that God operates in ways that are beyond our comprehension. God offers wisdom and understanding in trying situations. Make sure trusting in His unchanging nature.

Today, reflect on how God's constancy offers a stable basis, particularly in the face of difficult circumstances. Investigate how you can take refuge in God's goodness and constancy. Putting your faith in God through trials results in a haven in His protection and how Christ has never changed. Think about how Christ's steadfastness serves as an anchor, providing a solid foundation when things get hard. As you wrap up this devotional, consider how certain His purpose is. Think about God's promise to provide security, hope, and prosperity for the future despite whatever challenges you may encounter today.

Reflection:

Think back to a current struggle you are facing in your life. In the face of challenges, how may giving over control to God's greater viewpoint provide clarity and peace?

Prayer:

Almighty God, please let me see Your ways. Please help me to put my faith in Your wisdom, especially in situations that I cannot fully comprehend.

"For my thoughts are not your thoughts, neither are your ways my ways, declares the Lord." - Hebrews 55:8 (ESV).

"Your encounters with God have an impact on other people's lives, much as pondering ripples. The waves of His grace as you go into the depths of faith produce a transforming current that pulls people toward the Source of unending love."

Recognize that you are a living testimony because of your interactions with God as you begin this spiritual journey. Consider how you can demonstrate God's goodness to others via your life. Think back on the abundant happiness that results from your encounters with God. Visualize how the happiness and tranquility you experience today can benefit people around you.

Examine the results of empathy and compassion based on your encounters with God, also how the forgiveness of God in your own life can encourage compassion and forgiveness in your interpersonal connections now. Think about how changing your relationships with other people to reflect the perspective of Christ might have a revolutionary effect. As you wrap up this devotional, concentrate on the love that radiates from your encounters with God. Think about how the affection you get from Him can spill out and impact the lives of people surrounding you today.

Reflection:

Go back to a recent encounter with God. In what ways could your deeds and dispositions illuminate His light for people around you?

Prayer:

Lord, grant that my life serves as a constant reminder of Your goodness. Please assist me in illuminating You in an act that exalts You.

"Let your light shine before others, that they may see your good deeds and glorify your Father in heaven." - Matthew (NIV) 5:16

Day 16

"With the direction of the Holy Spirit, humanity becomes an enlightened path where each action is filled with divine meaning, and the path beyond is made clear by an illumination of eternal wisdom."

Start this devotional by recognizing the gift of the Holy Spirit as your heavenly leader. The promise that God the Father sends the Holy Spirit to instruct and reaffirm God's wisdom to you. May the power of the Holy Spirit as the truth-illuminating force. Think about how the Spirit helps you comprehend God's truth more fully. Examine the Holy Spirit's quiet, little whisper.

How God frequently communicates to you in quiet times? Guiding you with a soft hand and the presence of the Holy Spirit as your own personal advisor. Think about how God's Word contains wisdom, and how the Spirit's job is to impart it and convince you of it today. As you wrap up this devotional, pay close attention to placing your trust in the Holy Spirit to guide you. Think on the promise that God's Word illuminates your path today, led by the Spirit.

Reflection:
Think back to a recent choice you made or circumstance you sought advice on. In what ways could accepting the guidance of the Holy Spirit as your heavenly mentor offer comfort and assurance?

Prayer:
May the Holy Spirit lead me. As I make decisions in life, teach me, and inform me of the knowledge provided in God's Word.

"But the Advocate, the Holy Spirit, whom the Father will send in my name, will teach you all things and will remind you of everything I have said to you." - NIV John 14:26

"Searching for God's direction when making choices is a purposeful dialogue with God, asking His guidance to shine upon an area filled with confusion and create a path that follows the direction of His perfect purpose."

Give God complete control over your decision-making process to start this devotional. Consider the freedom that comes from putting your faith in God's wisdom rather than your own. Considering the assurance of divine guidance. Today, meditate on the promise that the Lord, in His love, gives advice and instruction to those who ask for it.

Analyze the significance of patience when making decisions. Contemplate the value of waiting on God for direction and timing today. Consider the suggestion to use prayer to determine God's will. Now focus on how seeking wisdom from God can help you make decisions that are clear. Concentrate on putting your faith in God's omnipresence as you wrap up this devotional. Assess the trust that keeps you going right now, even in the face of uncertainty.

Reflection:
Go back to a choice you are currently having to make. How may serenity and assurance come from giving the process up to God?

Prayer:
Heavenly Father, I give You wisdom in making this choice. Direct my actions and show me the proper path.

"Trust in the Lord with all your heart and lean not on your own understanding; in all your ways submit to him, and he will make your paths straight."
- NIV Proverbs 3:5–6

Day 18

"Setting up a prayer lifestyle is like establishing a place of refuge for the inner being, where each encounter with God develops an invisible thread flowing through the structure of your days, connecting together times of love and peace."

God invites you to pray and connect with Him in the cadence of your everyday life. Think about how beautiful it is to enter God's presence today and engage in a meaningful conversation. Accept the invitation to pray continuously. Think about how having everyday conversations with God can change your life today. Examine the effectiveness of fervent prayer.

Think on the promise that God hears and answers His children's sincere pleas. Consider the assurance that comes from pursuing God's will via prayer. Today, focus on how your faith in His responses is strengthened when your petitions are in line with His purposes. As you wrap up this devotional, remember how joyful it is to express gratitude in prayer. During your talks with God, consider how appreciation might improve your life.

Reflection:
Go back to a time when prayer seemed genuine and personal. In what ways may accepting prayer as a request strengthen your relationship with God?

Prayer:
Heavenly Father, I am grateful for the ability to pray. Allow Your invitation to enter my heart so that I can have constant communication with You.

"Devote yourselves to prayer, being watchful and thankful." - NIV Colossians 4:1–2.

"Forgiveness is a wonderful tapestry that is richly woven throughout God's plan. Every deed of reconciliation and forgiving is a step on the divine path that demonstrates the transformational potential of love in His exquisite plan."

Ground yourself in the premise of God's forgiveness to start this devotional. Consider the breadth of God's pardon provided to you in Christ. Contemplate on the mutual aspect of absolution. Now think about how forgiveness goes hand in hand with releasing forgiveness.

Discover the freedom that comes with letting go. Observe the weightlessness that results from pardoning others, just as the Lord pardoned you, today. Consider the therapeutic effects of forgiving. Today, think about the mental and spiritual healing that comes from forgiving yourself and others. As this devotional comes to an end, consider forgiveness as an expression of God's love. Consider how God's forgiveness reflects how much He loves you.

Reflection:
Go back to a time when you felt forgiven by God. How could realizing the basis of His pardon motivate you to show others grace?

Prayer:
Almighty God, I am grateful for the pardon that is found in Christ. Allow the transformational power of sharing that grace with others to enter my heart.

"Be kind and compassionate to one another, forgiving each other, just as in Christ God forgave you." - NIV Ephesians 4:32

Day 20

"The art of matching your heart with God's magnificent brushstrokes is pursuing His plan daily. Every step you take on this deliberate journey becomes a brushstroke, painting a picture of obedience and meaning on the canvas that is your life."

Start this devotional by recognizing that every day's dawn presents a chance to seek God's will. Think about the excitement of lining up your actions with His plan. See the force of a heart that is given up.

Think about the freedom you get when you give the Lord control over all your endeavors and let Him make your plans today. Investigate the option of praying for direction. Consider the assurance that God hears the sincere pleas of individuals who come to Him.

Consider how crucial it is to live according to God's Word. Today, reflect on how following His will requires you to line your activities with His directives. This devotional ends with an emphasis on trusting the timing of God. Contemplate the promise that waiting upon the Lord provides a clear way and newfound power.

Reflection:
Establish a morning habit that establishes your daily schedule. How may giving every moment purpose come from intentionally pursuing God's will?

Prayer:
Heavenly Father, please lead me and direct my heart as I begin this new day. May you live each minute seeking Your will.

"Trust in the Lord with all your heart and lean not on your own understanding; in all your ways submit to him, and he will make your paths straight."
- NIV Proverbs 3:5–6

"Confronting the road ahead with joy is not an absence of problems, but the presence of an attitude of gratitude that turns each turn, regardless of how rocky, into an act of faith—a triumph of the Lord who guides you along your path of purpose."

Take up the call to live a cheerful life to start this devotional. Consider the assurance that God shows you the way and extends an invitation to walk it joyfully. Take the suggestion to embrace the delight of the present. Think about how you may change your viewpoint today by choosing to rejoice in the day that the Lord has made. Examine the idea of happiness when facing difficulties. Consider the ability of joy to transform, even during adversity.

Evaluate the effects of bringing happiness to others. Look on how having a happy heart heals people around you as well as yourself. Contemplate the everlasting delight that can only be experienced through God's presence as you wrap up this devotional. Consider the assurance that there is an eternal abundance of delight in Him.

Reflection:
Think back to a recent instance that made you happy. How might adopting an optimistic outlook affect the way you approach the journey that lies ahead?

Prayer:
Almighty Father, I am deeply grateful for the opportunity to traverse life with joy. Let the joy all around me fill my eyes, and may it influence my path.

"You make known to me the path of life; in your presence, there is fullness of joy; at your right hand are pleasures forevermore." - Psalm 16:11 (ESV)

"How faith impacts the outcome of your life is the hidden power that transforms trials into possibilities failures into recoveries, and doubt into an experience of supernatural unfoldment—a testimony to the remarkable strength that comes from trusting in what is promised of God."

Start this devotional by learning about the basis of faith. Consider how faith is the foundation of a journey that transforms. As you wrap out this devotional, consider how faith may alter. Appreciate the amazing opportunities that faith presents to you now. Analyze how faith affects your ability to make decisions.

Believe of the way your decisions are shaped today by your faith in the Lord. Examine how faith can help you get over fear. Explore how confidence in God's promises inspires bravery and banishes fear today. Consider the transforming perspective that faith offers in the face of difficulties. Consider of how your response to challenging circumstances changes when you live by faith.

Reflection:
Think back to a previous instance where faith was important. What effect did believe in the invisible have on the result?

Prayer:
"Faithful Father, I firmly establish my journey on the rock of faith." May the results I experience be shaped by my faith in Your promises.

Hebrews 11, verse 1 (NIV): "Now faith is confidence in what we hope for and assurance about what we do not see."

"Serving others in God's love is like a compassionate symphony, with every unselfish note combining with the melody of heavenly grace. We resemble the soul of the Lord who first loved us when we give."

Examine your feelings to serve as you start this devotional. Consider how Jesus, the epitome of love, came to serve rather than to be served. Study the power of love to inspire service. Today, reflect on how serving others with a complete devotion to God transforms it into an act of love. Discover the delight of unselfish service offering. Note the delight that comes to both the giver and the recipient today, as well as the transformational power of cheerful giving.

Contemplate acts of compassion. Think about how serving others becomes a different experience when you dress yourself in the virtues of kindness, patience, humility, gentleness, and compassion. As this devotional comes to an end, concentrate on bearing testimony to God's love. Think about the great influence your deeds of kindness can have on people today showing them Christ's love.

Reflection:
Recall back to a moment in your life when you were touched by someone's unselfish service. In what ways did their behavior reflect the intentions of Christ?

Prayer:
"Loving Father, please show me the love and humility that Jesus demonstrated in his service." May I be motivated by His example to serve others with empathy.

"For even the Son of Man did not come to be served, but to serve, and to give his life as a ransom for many." - NIV Mark 10:45

"Reflecting on God's faithfulness is like to turning through the pages of a book with unshakable promises written in it. His faithfulness is seen in every chapter, and God consistency becomes the finished product that creates the representation of your grateful heart in the story of your life."

Explore the tenets of God's faithfulness to start this devotional. Consider today the promise that God's faithfulness is unending, and His love is limitless.

Observe the fidelity of God throughout all the seasons. Reflect on how His mercies and love, which are replenished every morning, help you get through life's ever shifting seasons.

Examine the immutable nature of God. Consider daily the steadfastness of His fidelity, rooted in the knowledge that Jesus Christ never changes. Examine your own personal accounts of God's faithfulness. Believe regarding how your life's reflection of His amazing accomplishments can serve as a testament to His magnificent glory today. As you wrap up this devotional, consider leaving a faithful legacy. Examine the assurance that individuals who put their trust in the Lord will be strengthened and protected in His faithfulness.

Reflection:
Think back to a moment when you were shown God's faithfulness. How did His perseverance come to be a cornerstone of your spiritual journey?

Prayer:
Dear God, I firmly ground my thoughts in Your steadfast love. May my behaviors and viewpoint be shaped by the foundations of Your faithfulness.

"Your love, Lord, reaches to the heavens, your faithfulness to the skies." - Psalm 36:5 (NIV)

"The effect of God's grace on the world is a result of your transformation. The constant reminders of His love build into a structure of light as you accept the change, He is creating inside you, encouraging others to look within for their own brilliant joy."

Examine the idea of metamorphosis at the beginning of this devotional. Consider the opportunity to transform yourself now by rethinking and stepping out of this world's patterns. See how you are a living example of God's transforming activity. Think about how this process of becoming into His likeness carries an increasing brightness that affects everyone around you now.

Examine how change affects relationships. Evaluate right now how your relationship with others has changed because of being a new creation in Christ. Think about the ways your faith has changed things at work. Believe regarding how your dedication to serving the Lord influences the people and environment in your work life today. As you wrap up this devotional, consider how your change has affected others. Think about how your changed life might radiate a light that honors your heavenly Father today.

Reflection:
Think back to a time when your life changed. What effects did mental renewal have on your outlook and decisions?

Prayer:
God, I renew myself and give myself over to Your power to change. May Your nice, pleasant, and perfect will be continuously regenerated in my thinking.

"Leave your old ways behind and allow your mind to be renewed in order to become transformed. It will then be possible for you to determine what God's will is—that is, his good, acceptable, and perfect will." —Romans 12:2 (NIV)

Day 26

"The art of living a purpose-driven life is lining up your goals with God's heavenly brushstrokes. Your path becomes a work of art with every deliberate step you take, bearing witness to the deep beauty that arises from fulfilling the reason of which you were specially created."

Start this devotional by talking about the idea of finding God's purpose. Think on the knowledge that God has deliberate plans for your life, plans that are full of hope and a future. Analyze how you can live in accordance with God's will. Today, reflect on how pursuing His righteousness and kingdom forms the cornerstone of leading a life that is motivated by purpose. Examine how purpose affects decisions you make every day.

Consider how giving your efforts and objectives to the Lord creates a direction that is intentional today. Try discovering meaning in hardship. Today, reflect on how God is still at work in your life, working for your benefit and His purpose, even during difficult circumstances. As you wrap out this devotional, consider leaving a purposeful legacy. Evaluate how living a life that is oriented around Jesus becomes the goal today, impacting both the here and now as well as eternity.

Reflection:
Think back to a moment when you had a feeling of direction. In what ways did the encounter fit into God's purposes for your life?

Prayer:
Father in heaven, please show me Your plan for my life. Let me see the plans You have created for me, plans that are full of promise and a future.

"For I know the plans I have for you, declares the Lord, plans for welfare and not for evil, to give you a future and a hope." - ESV Jeremiah 29:11

"Finding God in everyday life is like recognizing a holy place in the typical, where every moment becomes an opportunity for divine enlightenment, and everything around us transcends into an amazing representation of God presence."

Start this devotional by considering how close God is to us in our daily lives. Today, reflect on how God is ever-present and waiting to be encountered in life's everyday events. Imagine how much God cares about the specifics of your life. Thinking on how much of your day is under His loving and attentive supervision today.

Investigate seeking God's direction for daily choices. Take the knowledge that God gives you advice and direction while keeping a watchful eye on you. Recall how you have felt God's peace when facing difficulties. Think about how praying to God offers a serenity that is beyond comprehension now. As you wrap up this devotional, pay particular attention to acknowledging God's influence in the community. Consider the assurance that God is present in groups of Christians, providing chances for people to encounter Him via others.

Reflection:
Consider a recent instance in which you felt God was close to you. How has His presence changed the way you view the ordinary?

Prayer:
All-pervading God, let me see Your presence even in the ordinary. May I truly call upon You and feel Your presence with me in every situation.

"The Lord is near to all who call on him, to all who call on him in truth." - NIV Psalm 145:18

"Recognizing the strengths God's innumerable blessings is a form of thanksgiving, where each breath of thanks pours an outline of gratitude on a piece of your heart, forming an image of abundant grace."

Today devotional start by discussing the idea of having an appreciative heart. Consider God's kindness and unfailing love today; they should inspire gratitude. Examine the blessings you may find in everyday situations. Think about how God's immutable character is reflected in every good and flawless gift today. Assess the most important present of redemption.

Appreciate the major benefit of everlasting life via Christ today, and the thankfulness it engenders. Ponder the benefits of overcoming obstacles. Today, reflect on how God, despite adversity, works for the welfare of those who love Him. As you wrap up this devotional, concentrate on developing an attitude of gratitude. Consider the practice of giving your petitions to God with an attitude of appreciation.

Reflection:

Think back to a recent instance in which you were grateful to God. What effect does realizing His kindness have on your viewpoint?

Prayer:

Almighty God may my heart become receptive to thankfulness. I express my gratitude for Your unwavering love and goodness, which envelop me every day.

"Give thanks to the Lord, for he is good; his love endures forever." - NIV Psalm 107:1

"Be light in this dark world. Glow brightly in the dark with love, compassion, and unflinching faith. Your brightness has the capacity to chase away gloom and direct others toward the source of unending light."

Examine the invitation to be a light in the world as you start this devotional. Think on the affirmation that you are the world's light, meant to shine brightly, and give it some thought. Think back to the light's origin. Today, reflect on how walking in the light of

Jesus, the world's light, will guarantee that you dispel the darkness all around you.

Focus on the certainty that you possess Christ's light inside you, which is sufficient to drive out darkness. Accept the invitation to rise and shine. Think about the way your light shines the majesty of the Lord today, illuminating and radiating everyone in your vicinity. As you wrap out this devotional, concentrate on living forth your light. Consider how your good deeds bring God honor by serving as an outward manifestation of your inner light.

Reflection:
Think back to a moment when you experienced the influence of another person's light. In what ways might your life serve as a comparable source of inspiration for others?

Prayer:
Dear God, please assist me to accept my responsibility as a light in the world. May Your light shine brilliantly within me, banishing all shadows and offering hope.

"You are the world's light. You cannot hide a metropolis perched on a hill. Additionally, instead of lighting a lamp and placing it beneath a basket, they place it on a stand, which illuminates the entire home." Matthew 5:14–15, ESV

Day 30

"Fulfilling your deepest purpose in Christ is a holy vow to synchronize the desires of your heart with His divine plan, not merely a quest. Your passion turns into a symphony in this harmonic dance, exalting the One who planned all of your desires."

Let's begin today by discussing the idea of rediscovering Christ's passion. The encouragement to find joy in the Lord and the assurance that He will grant your heart's desires as you consider these things. Think about pursuing God's kingdom as the origin of genuine passion. Focus on how pursuing what is righteous in God's eyes leads to fulfillment and further gifts.

Examine the fervent quest for holiness. Analyze the call to holiness in behavior today and how it relates to your greatest desire for Christ. Consider discovering your special calling in Christ. Think about how God's planning and design reveal a unique purpose for you today, igniting your enthusiasm. As you wrap up this devotional, think about the notion of overflowing passion. Observe the relationship that exists today between happiness, serenity, and the abundant hope that results from a fervent conviction in Christ.

Reflection:
Think back to a time when your love for Christ was very alive. How might you spark that love and excitement for Him again?

Prayer:
Kindly, God, rekindle my inner fire of passion. May my joy in You be the source from which my heart's wishes are satisfied.

"Delight yourself in the Lord, and he will give you the desires of your heart." - Psalm 37:4 (ESV)

As we come to an end of our study of "Morning Blessings & Mercies: Fulfilling Your Walk in His Purpose," we are left with a deep sense of appreciation, mercies that never end, and the holy rhythm of divine purpose. Our lives are the pages of this trip, which plays out like a masterfully written novel with each dawn offering a fresh chance to walk hand in hand with God.

The Psalms are full with glimpses into David's heart. "I will give thanks to the Lord because of his righteousness; I will sing the praises of the name of the Lord Most High" (Psalm 7:17, emphasis added).

David's psalms were a song of thanksgiving, a poetic representation of a heart aware of the gifts that met every morning. Upon our conclusion, we bear the spirit of David, prepared to dance in the dawn, confessing the holiness of our Creator.

Embrace of Abraham's faith: the type of faith that, having confidence in God's promises, goes forth into the unknown. "By faith Abraham, when called to go to a place he would later receive as his inheritance, obeyed and went, even though he did not know where he was going" (Hebrews 11:8, emphasis added). Walking in Abraham's footsteps each morning, believing that every step we take will bring us closer to God's divine plan inheritance, is how we walk in His purpose.

Mary is seen to be accepting blessings with humility in her heart. "But the messenger of God said to her, 'Do not be afraid, Mary; you have found favor with God'" (1:30 in Luke). Mary had a moment of heavenly favor and kindness when she met the angel Gabriel. Like Mary, we remain in God's favor and are prepared to accept the graces that pour like a soothing stream with each dawn. In a same vein, our conclusion acknowledges this.

We might compare to the story of the Samaritan who went back to thank God for his cure. "'Were not all ten cleansed?' Jesus questioned. The remaining nine are where? Is this foreigner the only one who has returned to thank God?" (Luke 17–18). Our journey toward His goal entails taking up the Samaritan's attitude of thankfulness, which is returning the favor of acknowledging the morning's graces and bounties.

The resolution is consistent with Paul's statements of strong intent. "But one thing I do: Forgetting what is behind and straining toward what is ahead, I press on toward the goal to win the prize for which God has called me heavenward in Christ Jesus" (Philippians 3:13). Paul inspires us with his unwavering dedication to living a worthwhile life and his relentless pursuit of his objectives. We vow to be walking in His purpose with a forward-focused determination and letting go of the shadows of the past as we finish.

We see that the path Jesus Himself paved for us is one of submission, thankfulness, and intentional life. The words "Very early in the morning, while it was still dark, Jesus got up, left the house, and went off to a solitary place, where he prayed" (Mark 1:35) reverberate in our consciousness. In the footsteps of Jesus, our mornings become a holy retreat, a quiet space where we communicate with the divine.

We understand that it is only a beginning rather than the end of eternity. Every sunrise, every favor, and every act of kindness become brushstrokes in the magnificent painting that is our life. We face the future with palms wide out to accept mercies, a heart tuned to the melodies of thankfulness, and feet in line with His intention.

Our resolution to live a life filled with morning mercies and benefits is not just a contemplation. It's a promise to wake up with eyes open to see the mercies that are being revealed, a heart attuned to the murmurs of thankfulness, and actions in line with His plan. As a result, the ending is really a beginning –

the beginning of a life that is deeply entwined with the divine story.

The characters of David's thankfulness, Abraham's trust, Mary's humility, the Samaritan's thanks, Paul's intentional living, and Jesus' example are carried into the mornings that lie ahead of us as the curtain closes on our investigation. At the end, we will rejoice in the morning's gifts, give thanks for God's gentle mercies, and step purposefully into the path He has prepared for us. We greet each new day with hearts full of thanksgiving, eyes set on His promises, and a purposeful determination. It is a day full of His benefits, abundant mercies, and the realization of His divine purpose in our lives.

Every step we take is a note in a heavenly symphony in the magnificent fabric of life. Our trek is a holy dance of appreciation, trust, and surrender; it is a journey that is perfectly woven into the plan that the Creator has created. Our hearts are filled with the echo of His promises as we travel this trip, and we take comfort in the knowledge that each step is evidence of His plan coming to pass.

Gratitude is a lifestyle choice as well as a feeling. It is a fundamental aspect of our walk. It is a recognition of the many benefits that are all around us. We are encouraged to "Give thanks to him and praise his name; enter his gates with thanksgiving and his courts with praise" (Psalm 100:4). Gratitude turns into the gateway that opens to show the depth of His purpose for our lives, allowing us to enter the wide swath of His purpose.

Even in the darkest hours, the lamp of faith illuminates the way for us as we travel. "Faith is confidence in what we hope for and assurance about what we do not see," according to Hebrews 11:1. We go through the region of the invisible, believing that His promises provide a solid base on which to stand. Even in situations where the path ahead appears unclear, faith serves as the compass that points us in the direction of His plan.

Surrendering is a source of strength rather than a sign of weakness on our journey. Proverbs 3:5-6 tells us to "Trust in the Lord with all your heart and lean not on your own understanding; in all your ways submit to him, and he will make your paths straight." Giving up control and letting God's perfect plan guide us is what it means to consciously surrender. We find that His plan becomes clear and purposeful when we yield.

Every morning serves as a canvas for the grace-filled image that is created by His favors. We are reminded in Lamentations 3:22–23, "We are not devoured by the Lord's tremendous love because his compassions never fail. They are fresh every morning; your loyalty is amazing." The gifts of the morning serve as a preamble to the meaningful day that lies ahead, serving as a prompt that God's mercies never end at sunrise and an invitation to carry out His will every instant, we are awake.

Isaiah 30:21 states, "Whether you turn to the right or to the left, your ears will hear a voice behind you, saying, 'This is the way; walk in it.'" This is our call to obedience as we pursue His purpose. Rather than being a narrow road, obedience is a doorway that opens to the vastness of His plan. Our stroll becomes a monument to the elegance of lining up our steps with His heavenly direction as we pay attention to His voice.

There are seasons of waiting and seasons of flowering in the garden that is our lives. "There is a time for everything, and a season for every activity under the heavens," according to Ecclesiastes 3:1. Our walk in His plan recognizes that waiting is a time of preparation rather than stagnation. When we wait patiently, we find that He has perfect time and that He is the one who orchestrates every blossoming season.

Our stroll is a group dance rather than a lonely excursion. The power of community is highlighted in Ecclesiastes 4:9–10, where it is said that "two are better than one because they have a good return for their labor: If either of them falls down, one can help the other up." Walking with other pilgrims gives our journey more resiliency and encouragement. We encourage one another while discussing the pleasures and difficulties of accomplishing His goal.

Paul's tenacity serves as a light for us and an encouragement to bear with hardships. He says, "I have kept the faith, I have finished the race, and I have fought the good fight" in 2 Timothy 4:7. Even if there will be obstacles on our path, perseverance gives us the willpower to continue. Every step serves as a testament to the persistence of faith and the accomplishment of His plan.

When we keep our gaze fixed on the eternal, our trek takes on new meaning. Paul exhorts us in Colossians 3:2 to "set your minds on things above, not on earthly things." This everlasting viewpoint serves as a beacon that points the way toward heavenly goals. We discover the sacred in the ordinary; we catch a glimpse of the eternal in the temporal, and our stroll turns into a sublime voyage beyond of space and time.

We understand that this reflection on walking in His plan is only the beginning rather than the end. Every remark said and every verse read serves as a call to begin the next phase of our life with a fresh sense of purpose. Our path is a story that never ends—a tale of thankfulness, faith, surrender, morning gifts, obedience, patience, fellowship, and an everlasting outlook.

May every step be a dance, every dawn an occasion to celebrate, and every deed done with intention a note in the orchestra of His perfect design. Let us, as we come to an end, weave these thoughts into the fabric of our days, walking in His purpose with eyes set on His promises, a heart attuned to His guidance, and steps in step with the everlasting pattern He has planned.

An invitation to become closer to the Divine and walk hand in hand with the universe's creator is echoed in the gentle call that is present in the ups and downs of life. Rather than perfection, this path is characterized by a genuine yearning to know and be known by the One who painstakingly crafted every strand of our existence.

The invitation to be closer to God is a soft murmur that invites us to establish a stronger bond rather than being an order. This promise is found in James 4:8: "Draw near to God, and he will draw near to you." This assurance that the Creator of galaxies leans in when we move near Him reverberates through the passageways of our hearts.

The soul converses with its Creator through prayer. "Do not be anxious about anything, but in everything by prayer and supplication with thanksgiving let your requests be made known to God," Philippians 4:6-7 tells us. And in Christ Jesus, your hearts and minds will be protected by the peace of God, which is greater than human comprehension." We discover a haven where anxieties vanish and serenity becomes our constant companion when we pray.

Through prayer, the soul converses with its Creator. Philippians 4:6-7 gives us encouragement: "Do not be worried about anything; instead, make all of your requests known to God through prayer and petition, with thankfulness. And in Christ Jesus, the peace of God, which is more than human comprehension, will keep watch over your hearts and minds. We discover a haven of calm in prayer, where anxieties fade and serenity becomes our constant companion.

Amidst life's noise, quiet times are treasured. It is gently urged to "be still, and know that I am God" in Psalm 46:10. We have a profound contact with the Divine in the quiet solitude, receiving comfort, clarity, and a fresh awareness of His presence.

Creation turns into a canvas on which God's fingerprints are clearly seen. According to Romans 1:20, "For his invisible attributes, namely, his eternal power and divine nature, have been clearly perceived, ever since the creation of the world, in the things that have been made." We experience the craftsmanship of the Creator in the dance of sunshine and the rustling of leaves, which draws us nearer to His heart.

God's unfailing love is portrayed in Zephaniah 3:17, which says, "The Lord your God is in your midst, a mighty one who will save; he will rejoice over you with gladness; he will quiet you by his love; he will exult over you with loud singing." We discover acceptance, atonement, and a love that is beyond our understanding in the warmth of His affection.

It is inevitable that we will endure trials and tribulations, but when we confront them with faith, they become stepping stones rather than obstacles. Recall that James 1:2–4 says, "My brothers, count it all joy when you face trials of all kinds, because you know that the trying of your faith produces steadfastness." And let constancy to work its magic so that you might be flawless and whole, needing nothing."

Our religion is homed in a school setting created by adversity. According to Romans 5:3-5, "Not only that, but we rejoice in our sufferings, knowing that suffering produces endurance, and endurance produces character, and character produces hope, and hope does not put us to shame, because God's love has been poured into our hearts through the Holy Spirit who has been given to us."

The unmerited gift of grace is emphasized in Ephesians 2:8–9: "For it is by grace that you have been saved through faith." Furthermore, so that nobody may take credit for it, this is a gift from God rather than the product of your efforts. His grace surrounds us in our moments of weakness, reassuring us that we are loved beyond measure.

Suffering turns into a sign of our loyalty and God's constant presence. Hebrews 10:23 gives us encouragement, saying, "Let us hold fast the confession of our hope without wavering, for he who promised is faithful." Our tenacity creates a symphony that echoes in the sky, a reflection of His constancy.

Holy Spirit becomes our consoling and guiding spirit. According to John 14:26, "But the Helper, the Holy Spirit, whom the Father will send in my name, he will teach you all things and bring to your remembrance all that I have said to you." We may hear the Holy Spirit guiding us in the soft murmurs and nudgings, bringing us nearer to God's perfect will.

Gratitude turns into a tune that aligns our hearts with the frequency of God. "Rejoice always, pray without ceasing, give thanks in all circumstances; for this is the will of God in Christ Jesus for you," is an encouraging verse found in 1 Thessalonians 5:16–18. Joy is found in thankfulness, and joy serves as a conduit to God's heart.

In a society where criticism is common, choosing love becomes revolutionary. According to Matthew 22:39, "And a second is like it: You shall love your neighbor as yourself." As a mirror of the love God pours into our lives, love becomes the cornerstone of our connections.

1 John 1:5 says, "This is the message we have heard from him and proclaim to you, that God is light, and in him is no darkness at all." Living in God's light

entails being honest, upright, and dedicated to bringing our lives into line with His word.

When we firmly ground ourselves on God's promises, fear begins to fade. The verse 41:10 says to us, "Fear not, for I am with you; be not dismayed, for I am your God; I will strengthen you, I will help you, I will uphold you with my righteous right hand." Fear fades in His presence and is replaced with a steadfast confidence in His safety.

Giving up control is a sign of faith in the One who oversees the universe. Proverbs 3:5–6 instructs us to "Lean not on your own understanding but put all of your trust in the Lord." Recognize him in all of your endeavors, and he will make your pathways straight." Giving in opens the door to divine alignment.

Our hymn is Philippians 3:14, "I press on toward the goal for the prize of the upward call of God in Christ Jesus." Notwithstanding the difficulties, we have our sights set on the goal—the upward call of God—which gives us the fortitude and hope to move ahead.

Let these words reverberate throughout the rooms as we consider our journey toward being closer to God.

A 30-DAY DEVOTIONAL ON THE GOSPEL FULFILLING YOUR WALK IN HIS PURPOSE
Morning
Blessing
&
&Mercies
BY; TONY MEJIA

www.ingramcontent.com/pod-product-compliance
Lightning Source LLC
Chambersburg PA
CBHW052122150726

48002CB00006B/2449